Smart Macros Low Carb Cookbook: 50 Recipes and a 30 Day Meal Plan For Weight Loss, Carb Reduction, and a Healthier You

Disclaimer and Terms of Use: Effort has been made to ensure that the information in this book is accurate and complete, however, the author and the publisher do not warrant the accuracy of the information, text and graphics contained within the book due to the rapidly changing nature of science, research, known and unknown facts and internet. The Author and the publisher do not hold any responsibility for errors, omissions or contrary interpretation of the subject matter herein. This book is presented solely for motivational and informational purposes only.

Table of Contents

Living the Low Carb Lifestyle

The Meaning of a Low Carb Lifestyle

A low carb diet is one that encourages people to eat a high amount of good quality proteins, fats, and fresh vegetables while at the same time dramatically reducing the amount of carbohydrates in the diet. This type of diet was created to foster fast weight loss and also to restore health, since high levels of carbohydrate and sugary foods have been linked to insulin imbalance and an increased risk for developing diseases like diabetes, heart disease, and cancer. When it comes to weight loss, low carb diets work because the body goes into "fat-burning" mode, using up existing stored body fat for energy whenever a very low amount of carbohydrate foods are being consumed.

Following the Standard American Diet (commonly referred to as "SAD") usually means people are getting between 40-70% of their daily calories from carbohydrate foods. A low carb diet in contrast encourages people to get only around 10-15% of their calories from carbs, while the rest come from mainly proteins, fats, and non-starchy vegetables.

The exact amount of carbs encouraged on a low carb diet really depends on the specific kind that is being followed and how quickly someone wants to see weight-loss results. There are a range of low carb diets that are promoted today, some that encourage people to follow the diet plan for only several weeks or in stages (like the Atkins Diet), while others encourage people to adapt the low carb diet as a lifestyle long-term (like the Paleo Diet).

Low carb diets that also keep general health in mind encourage people to eat real, whole, unprocessed low carb foods. A food is considered low carb when it contains low, or no, levels of starch and sugar. Eating low amounts of carbohydrates forces the body to rely on using its "fat storage" reserves for energy and body functioning, as opposed to the body using carbs from food.

The purpose behind a healthy low carb diet is not only to foster weight loss, but to reduce cravings for high sugar and starch foods, to restore appropriate insulin and blood sugar levels, to improve energy, and to decrease the likelihood of developing serious illnesses due to the harmful effects of high processed carb and sugar levels in the body.

Foods that are considered low carb- like meat, non-starchy vegetables, and healthy fats- almost all have low scores on the "glycemic index", which is a fancy way of saying that the foods are absorbed into the blood stream more slowly and won't result in a sudden surge of sugar in the blood. Blood sugar spikes are harmful and unpleasant because they can lead to health problems like metabolic syndrome, diabetes, hypoglycemia and weight gain, plus they can leave you feeling groggy, craving even more carbs, and on an emotional rollercoaster in terms of energy levels.

Foods that are not considered low carb are those that have high levels of sugar, starch, and are lacking protein and healthy fats, thus they have a more dramatic impact on your blood sugar levels. It is very easy for many people to become somewhat "addicted" to carbohydrate foods, because the sugar present in all carbs has a reaction in the "reward center" of our brains, comparable to how certain drugs make us feel; they leave us with a sense of happiness and pleasure, however this affect is only temporary. Soon afterwards, the good feelings dissipate and we are left wanting even more sugar from carbohydrate foods.

This is the reason many people experience cravings for high sugar and starch foods in all forms: bread, pasta, cookies, cake, and even fruit. The more a person eats these types of foods, the more they are reinforcing the habit and programming their brains to keep craving more.

To understand which foods contain the most carbohydrates and sugars in them, let's look at this list below of the foods with the most carbs (organized in order based on portion size, starting with the most carbs/sugar and decreasing):

Sugars, syrups & sweeteners
Candy
Soda or juice

Jams, jellies, preserves
Dried fruit
Snacks like potato chips and cakes/crackers
Cookies or cakes
Processed flours (white flour, rice flour, potato flour, etc)
Breads, toast, bagels, pizza, muffins, pitas, rolls, other baked goods
Potatoes

Here is the opposing list of foods with the least amount of sugar/carbs (all contain practically zero carbs):

All meat products
All chicken/poultry
All fish
Most fats like oils, butter, lard
Non starchy vegetables
Vinegars and sugar free condiments like mustard
Spices and herbs
Most full fat cheeses
Heavy cream or mayonnaise
Coffee and tea

So how exactly do low carb diets work?

When someone is on a low carb diet they avoid foods that contain most forms of sugars and starches: most fruits, grains, sweeteners like sugar or honey, most starchy vegetables, and all processed carbohydrates like bread, pasta, and cereal. *Insulin* is the hormone that is responsible for balancing blood sugar levels when someone does eat these types of foods, so when a person eats a low carb diet, they maintain low insulin levels.

The absence of sugars and starches allows the blood sugar to stabilize and the levels of insulin in the blood, which is a *fat storing* hormone, to drop significantly. A lower level of insulin increases the *fat burning* ability. The opposite is also true- the more the body needs to pump out insulin as a result of eating a high amount of sugar and starches, the more fat storing that usually takes place. "Insulin resistance", a harmful condition that is becoming more prevalent, occurs when someone's cells become "numb" to the effects of insulin, meaning even more insulin is needed to keep a balance of blood sugar. The higher the level of insulin in someone's blood, the more insulin resistant they are.

Low carb diets also usually make people consume less calories overall, since the types of foods that they are eating in place of carbohydrates make them feel very full, thus these foods are difficult to over eat and "binge" on. Low carb foods like steak, bacon, and eggs are filing foods because they contain high amounts of protein and fat, which the body takes a long time to break down and digest.

Where most carbohydrates do not fill us up for very long, leaving us hungry for more food shortly after, high fat and protein foods do the opposite- they turn off our hunger signals via the hormones that the brain releases after consuming them. High carb foods like fruit, pasta, and bread normally do the opposite when it comes to our hunger- they are not able to keep us full for very long and we find we are able to consume large amounts of them at one time before we feel that we've eaten enough.

Let's look at more detail of how carbohydrates are processed by the body and turned into fat:

All foods containing carbohydrates are broken down into simple sugars in the intestines. The sugar is then absorbed into the blood stream, which raises the blood sugar, or "glucose", levels. This increases the production of insulin; remember when you hear increased insulin, think "fat storing". Insulin prevents fat burning and stores extra calories from food as fat cells.

This is why it's very important to not consume too many calories for your body over time, because this will lead to an increase in the amount of fat cells present. Someone is a lot more likely to over-consume calories when they eat low protein, low fat, high carb foods that leave them feeling hungry and also increase food cravings.

Foods that spike insulin levels tend to make us hungry and not satisfied for very long, so we look for more food quickly after eating them. This creates a cycle of eating high carb foods and subsequently wanting even higher carb foods. You can see where this is going: a cycle is formed where eating carbs leads to eating even more carbs. This leads to overeating of calories in general and weight gain for many people.

On the other hand, a low amount of carbs from food gives us a more stable level of glucose (sugar) in the blood stream, which lowers the amount of insulin we produce. Remember, when you hear lower insulin, think "fat burning". Low insulin increases the release of fat from your body's fat stores and facilitates fat burning for energy. This usually leads to quick weight loss for people eating a low carb diet, especially if someone has a lot of weight to lose and is considered obese or quite overweight with a high amount of previously stored fat available.

All of the foods that are included in a *healthy* low carb diet will have these characteristics in common:

- Lower carbohydrate intake and lower glycemic index score
- Low sugar, low starch
- Higher protein intake
- Moderate to higher fat intake dominated by monounsaturated and polyunsaturated fats
- High intake of, vitamins, minerals, antioxidants, and plant phytochemicals

Although you will find a more detailed list of recommended low carb recipes later in this book, to give you an idea of what to expect, here is an example of what a few days on a low carb diet would look like for you:

- Breakfast: 2 Egg Omelet (including yolks) with vegetables, made using healthy oil or good quality butter.

- Lunch: Large mixed salad with grilled chicken or fish, a small amount of blueberries, and a handful of almonds.

- Dinner: Cheeseburger (with no bun), served with vegetables and more salad if you'd like.

- Snack: small amount of berries, nuts, protein source like full-fat yogurt or a piece of cheese

A ketogenic diet is one that follows the same basic principles of a low carb diet: it limits the amount of carbs, sugar, and starches entering the body and replaces these things with high fat and high protein foods. Following a ketogenic diet forces the body to use another source of energy besides glucose (sugar from carbs) for body functioning. When no glucose is present in the body, the liver will burn fat molecules instead. These fat molecules (called acetoacetate and hydroxybutyrate) are known as "ketones". Most ketogenic diets severely limit the amount of carbs that make up the diet; usually they encourage people to get around just 2-5% of their total daily calories from carbohydrates.

As we've been discussing, when the body is running low on glucose, it uses fat stores for "fuel" instead. The more the body burns fat for energy, the more "ketone bodies" it produced. At the same time that ketone bodies increase in the body, blood sugar levels drop; these two have an inverse relationship with one another. As blood sugar (glucose) drops and consequently ketone body levels rise, the body experiences what is called "nutritional ketosis."

Most ketogenic diets promote eating high amounts of fats even more so than high amounts of protein. A typical ketogenic meal would include an appropriate amount of protein (not an unlimited amount) from a source like beef, eggs, or chicken, plus a source of natural fat (for example oil, butter, or natural fat from meat), plus some non-starchy vegetables (not potatoes or squash, but vegetables like leafy greens, broccoli, peppers, tomatoes, etc.)

The ketogenic affect sometimes gets a bad reputation because ketones can sometimes rise to a very high level with patients who have uncontrollable type 1 diabetes. However, most researchers believe that the level of ketones in someone's body after they have been following a low carb diet is much less than it is in someone's body who has type 1 diabetes.

Researchers who support a low carb diet do not feel that the level of ketones in the body from this dietary approach are harmful; they believe ketone production is a natural mechanism that the body produces when it is faced with low levels of carbs and sugar but it needs a source of energy. The body burning ketones for energy is an adaptive mechanism that is believed to have evolved thousands of years ago when people had to "fast" for days at a time due to scare amounts of food being available. Supporters of "nutritional ketosis" believe that this natural process can be used to help the body improve conditions such as diabetes, heart disease, auto-immune disease, Alzheimer's' disease, gluten intolerance, and more, although there is still research needed on long-term safety and benefits of ketosis.

A low carb diet may be appropriate for you if you experience any of these symptoms somewhat often or these descriptions sound like you:

- You need to lose weight, especially quickly
- You would like to improve, or ward off, a health condition related to managing your blood sugar levels (obesity, diabetes, metabolic syndrome, hypoglycemia, etc.)
- You feel a lack in energy, especially in the afternoon when you feel a "slump"
- You have feelings of dependence on and cravings for high carb and sugar foods
- You haven't been successful on other diet plans because you did not want to count calories or watch portions very closely
- You feel that you lack willpower to stop eating when you should be "full", portion control is an issue for you
- You are someone who likes eating high protein and high fat foods like bacon, eggs, cheese
- You are someone who feels you could go without carbohydrate foods once you got the hand of it
- You do not give into peer pressure very easily and do not mind "standing out" from the crowd in regards to the foods you choose to eat

People who are successful at losing weight on low carb diets love this approach to eating because a low carb diet requires no calorie counting, measuring food portions, no strange meal replacements, and also no feelings of "going hungry". Perhaps the two biggest perks of a low carb diet are that they keep you feeling very satiated since low-carb, high protein and fat foods tend to be very filling, and secondly that weight loss usually happens quickly compared to other diets.

So, pros of a low carb diet would include:

- Weight loss, usually happening quickly
- Decreased risk for developing serious conditions like diabetes, metabolic syndrome, auto-immune disease, and more
- No feelings of hunger since food is filling
- No need to count calories as long as you stick with low carb approved foods
- Ability to eat as much low starchy vegetables as you want if you are still hungry after a meal
- Increased energy levels, avoidance of mood swings
- Decrease in the amount of food cravings you experience
- Noticeable appearance in terms of your looks, you may appear more awake, thinner, and have a "glow"

Each person reacts differently to a low carb diet; some take to it very easily and find that they feel great almost immediately, while others struggle a bit more. Normally the more dependent someone is on carbohydrate foods, the more difficult it will be for them to give these foods up. However, most negative feelings resulting from a low carb diet usually go away with some time.

It's also important to realize that many of the potential cons of eating low carb are actually psychological affects and not physiological ones, meaning food cravings and feelings of deprivation may be the most negative things you experience when eating this way. These feelings too normally go away with some practice and time, as you get more comfortable eating this way and are motivated by the great results you see.

And potential cons of a low carb diet would include:

- Initial cravings for carbohydrate foods, especially sugary treats like candy, cookies, chocolate
- Feelings of low energy especially initially, although these usually decrease quickly for most people
- Needing to avoid many common foods at restaurants, parties, etc. and instead to only stick with low carb offerings
- Possible feelings of deprivation since many carbs like bread and pasta tend to be some of people's favorites
- Potentially spending more money on groceries since protein foods can be expensive at times

Lifestyle – Not a Diet

Protein Shopping List

Dairy	Poultry	Powders	Red Meat	Seafood
Cottage Cheese	Chicken breast	Egg	Extra-lean ground beef	Canned salmon in water
Egg whites	Chicken thighs	Legume	Ground buffalo	Salmon fillets
Non-fat Greek yogurt	Duck breast	Soy (try to avoid)	Low-sodium roast beef	Shellfish (crab, clams, lobster, shrimp, and scallops)
	Turkey breast	Whey	Cube Steak	Canned tuna in water
	Lean ground turkey		Flank Steak	Tuna fillets
	Low-sodium deli turkey		Round Steak	White-Fleshed fish
			Elk	

Carbohydrates Shopping List

Bread	Cereal	Fruit	Grains	Pasta	Root Veggies	Starch Veggies	Legumes
Whole grain	Bran	Apples	Barley	Brown rice pasta	Potatoes	Peas	Low-sodium beans
Ezekiel Bread	Fiber One	Apricots	Buckwheat	Whole grain pasta	Sweet potatoes	Corn	Lentils
Ezekiel English muffins	Granola	Bananas	Couscous				
Brown rice tortillas		Berries	Popcorn				
Corn tortillas		Grapes	Quinoa				
Ezekiel tortillas		Kiwi	Long grain brown rice				
		Melons	Wild rice				
		Oranges					
		Peaches					

		s					
		Pears					
		Pineap ple					
		Plums					

Veggies Shopping List

Asparagus	Beets	Broccoli	Carrots
Celery	Cabbage	Cauliflower	Collard Greens
Cucumber	Eggplant	Mushrooms	Onions
Lettuce	Mixed Greens	Green Beans	Peppers
Spinach	Sprouts	Squash	Tomatoes
Zucchini	Turnips		

Drinks Shopping List

Unsweetened Almond Milk	Coffee	Water	Tea	

Taste and Seasoning Shopping List

Dressin gs	Herbs	Liqui ds	Tomat o- Based	Pastes	Sweetene rs
Balsami c vinaigret te	Basil	Butter spray	Marina ra sauce	Chili paste	Stevia
Fat free salad dressing	Cayenne Pepper	Low- sodiu m	Salsa	Hummus (low-fat, in	

21

		chicken broth		moderation)	
	Chili powder	Chili sauce	Tomato paste	Mustard	
	Cinnamon	Lemon juice	Tomato sauce		
	Cloves	Lime juice			
	Cocoa powder	Soy sauce			
	Curry	Tabasco			
	Garlic	Franks red hot sauce			
	Ginger				
	Horseradish				
	Mrs. Dash Spices				
	Nutmeg				
	Oregano				
	Parsley				
	Paprika				
	Pepper				
	Sea salt				
	*Almost every spice is viable in moderation				

Fats Shopping List

Dairy	Dressings	Fruit	Seeds	Oils
Low fat cheese	Balsamic vinaigrette	Avocado	Almonds	Canola oil
Egg yolks	Low fat salad dressing	Olives	Almond butter	Fish oil
Feta cheese			Natural peanut butter	Flaxseed oil
Low fat Mozzarella cheese			Peanuts	Olive oil
			Pecans	Coconut oil
			Pumpkin seeds	
			Sunflower seeds	
			Walnuts	

Foods to Avoid Like the Plague

If you have any of the foods I am about to list, you need to get rid of them and avoid them like the plague. They WILL destroy your diet immediately, and they're not worth it, trust me.

- Alcohol
- Beer
- Chips
- Chocolate
- Candy
- Cookies
- Crackers
- Flour
- Fried foods
- Frozen dinners

- Juice
- Ice Cream
- Soda
- Sugar
- Syrup (Maple)
- Wine
- White Rice

If you are trying to lose weight, portioning your meals is essential. This is where SmartMacro gets the term "Macro" from. Instead of counting carbs, we're counting our macros. Below you will find a chart of how much of each macronutrient you want at each meal.

Carbs	Your serving of carbohydrates should be the size of a clenched fist.	
Protein	Your serving of protein should be the size and thickness of your palm.	
Fats	Your serving of fats should be no more than from the base of your thumb to the tip.	
Veggies	Your serving of veggies should be approximately two clenched fists, but feel free to overdo this one.	
Flavorings (Sauces, etc)	Your flavorings (sauces, spices, etc) should be no greater than two fingers. The less flavoring, the better for your body, the worse for your taste buds.	

A low carb diet may take some getting used to as you give up foods that are so commonly present in society today and that may have been some of your favorites in the past. But eating in a low carb way is like building a muscle; the more you flex it and work at improving it, the easier it gets.

You will likely come up with your own tricks and food substitutions that you find work well for you; keep note of these so you can keep practicing them and building up your low carb eating habits. While at first you may experience some cravings for carbs, sugars, and starches or feel a lack of energy initially, you will likely get over these feelings pretty quickly, normally within a couple of weeks.

You do not need to feel deprived when on a low carb diet; in fact, you may start cooking more and find that you enjoy experimenting in your kitchen and trying new low carb foods that you previously had never eaten before. If you commit to trying to prepare more of your own meals, you can experiment with many different healthy low carb food substitutions that you will find make the process of transitioning away from carb foods more easy. An example of some healthy low carb substitutions are: using almond or coconut flour in place of wheat flour when you bake, using large collard or lettuce leaves to make "wraps" instead of using bread or grain wraps, grating or spiralizing vegetables like zucchinis and carrots to create "noodles" instead of having regular pasta.

The exact amount of carbs to include in your diet depends on several factors like how much weight you need to lose, how quickly you want to lose weight, and how extreme you want to take your low carb way of eating (how willing you are to cut out all carb sources). Most low carb diets will recommend you aim to eat about 30-50 grams of carbs per day, or possibly even less initially. The Atkins Diet for example starts people off eating about 20 grams of carbs per day, which is extremely low, however after 2 weeks the amount is allowed to increase if the person wishes.

Eating 30 grams of carbs would be about the equivalent of having 2 pieces of fruit, or the equivalent of having many servings of non-starchy vegetables throughout the day. It would also be equivalent to having about 2 small pieces of bread or less, however this doesn't mean you can eat 2 pieces of bread when on a low carb diet, because you need to take into account the amount of carbs present in the other foods that you will be eating, like vegetables. Even though vegetables are low in carbs, they still do contain some in small amounts, so this is where low carb eaters are normally encouraged to get all of their carbs from, not from any grains or baked products.

According to the Atkins Diet, this is the carb count in many commonly eaten vegetables below. The net carb count equals the amount of carbs that are actually digested by the body, after taking into account fiber which is not digested as a carb. Fiber is not counted towards a food's carb count because essentially the body is not able to break it down and turn it into glucose/sugar; instead it remains intact and unbroken down while traveling through the digestive system. This is the reason fiber is important- it helps to facilitate proper digestive function. When someone does not eat enough fiber, which can happen somewhat commonly on a low carb diet due to a low level of grains and fruits, they may have trouble going to the bathroom. To make sure you eat enough fiber, plan to include many servings of vegetables each day since all vegetables contain fiber.

Vegetable	Serving Size/Prep	grams of net carbs
Alfalfa sprouts	½ cup/raw	0.2
Arugula	1 cup/raw	0.4
Bok choy	1 cup/raw	0.4
Celery	1 stalk	0.8

Chicory greens	½ cup/raw	0.1
Chives	1 tablespoon	0.1
Cucumber	½ cup	1.0
Daikon	½ cup	1.0
Endive	½ cup	0.4
Escarole	½ cup	0.1
Fennel	½ cup	1.8
Jicama	½ cup	2.5
Iceberg lettuce	1 cup	0.2
Mushrooms	½ cup	1.2
Parsley	1 tablespoon	0.1
Peppers	½ cup/raw	2.3
Radicchio	½ cup/raw	0.7
Radishes	6/raw	0.5
Romaine lettuce	1 cup	0.4
Artichoke	1/2 medium	3.5
Asparagus	6 spears	2.4
Artichoke hearts	1 canned	1.0
Avocados	½ whole (raw)	1.8
Bamboo shoots	½ cup	1.2

Broccoli	½ cup	1.7
Broccoli raw	½ cup	0.8
Broccoli rabe	½ cup	2.0
Broccoflower	½ cup	2.3
Brussels sprouts	¼ cup	1.8
Cabbage	½ cup (raw)	1.6
Cauliflower	½ cup (raw)	1.4
Swiss chard	½ cup	1.8
Collard greens	½ cup boiled	2.0
Eggplant	½ cup	2.0
Green String Beans	1 cup	4.1
Hearts of palm	1 heart	0.7
Kale	½ cup	2.4
Kohlrabi	¼ cup	2.3
Leeks	½ cup	3.4
Okra	½ cup	2.4
Olives green	5	0.1
Olives black	5	0.7
Onion	¼ cup	4.3
Pumpkin	¼ cup	2.4
Rhubarb	½ cup (unsweetened)	1.7

Sauerkraut	½ cup (drained)	1.2
Snow peas and snap peas in pod	½ cup with pods	3.4
Spaghetti squash	¼ cup boiled	2.0
Spinach	½ cup	2.2
Summer squash	½ cup	2.6
Tomato	¼ cup	4.3
Turnips	½ cup	3.3
Water chestnuts	¼ cup (canned)	3.5
Zucchini	½ cup	1.5

If you are not losing weight with a low carb diet that is moderately high in carbs (around 50 grams), you may wish to lower your carb intake to around 25 grams. This would likely require giving up all fruit, since fruit does contain sugar and therefore carbs.

You will want to continue consuming at least 20 grams of carbohydrates, even when on a low carb diet, because this amount is required for the body to function properly. This is still considered very "low carb" but ensures you are maintaining your health at the same time as losing weight.

When following a low carb diet plan, you will generally include and avoid the foods listed below.

Foods to Include:

Meats: Any type. This can include beef, pork, game meat, chicken, etc. It's best to choose organic or grass fed meat.

Fish and Shellfish: Any type. This can include salmon, mackerel, shrimp, lobster, scallops, etc.

Eggs: They can be cooked anyway. It's best to choose organic eggs.

Fats: This can include oils like coconut oil, olive oil, palm oil, or butter, nuts, seeds, and avocado.

Non-Starchy Vegetables: All kinds. This can include any leafy greens, all cabbage, cauliflower, broccoli, Brussels sprouts, asparagus, zucchini, eggplant, spinach, mushrooms, cucumber, lettuce, avocado, onions, peppers, tomatoes etc.

Dairy Foods: Always select full-fat options like real butter, cream (40% fat), sour cream, Greek/Turkish yogurt and high-fat cheeses. Avoid low fat or flavored kinds.

Nuts: all kinds. This can include almonds, cashews, peanuts, etc.

Berries: These are normally the only fruit allowed and are okay in small amounts. Other fruits that are sometimes allowed are low sugar varieties like grapefruit, kiwi, and honeydew melon.

Drinks: only water, seltzer, unsweetened coffee, unsweetened tea.

Foods to Avoid:

Foods with High Sugar Levels: soda, candy, juice, cookies, cake, sports drinks, ice cream, etc. Also avoid using added cane sugar or anything very sweet like honey and maple syrup.

Carbohydrate Foods: Breads, pastas, rice, potatoes, any grains. This even includes products that say they are "whole grain".

Starchy Vegetables: All vegetable "tubers"- a family of vegetables that grow under the ground- including potatoes, carrots, radishes, and beets, turnips, and parsnips.

Alcohol: All kinds should ideally be avoided, or only had in very small amounts

Fruit: All fruit is off limits except for berries on occasion in small amounts

Drinks: Anything with sugar added like soda, juice, or sweetened coffee and tea

It's best to limit your overall calorie intake as well as your carb intake, if you want to see fast weight loss results. For women, aiming for 1,400 calories every day is a good idea, while 1,600 for men is ideal. This would be an appropriate amount when quick weight loss is your goal. It is okay however to have more calories than this, it just means you will lose weight at a slower pace most likely. You can still lose weight in a gradual, healthy way when eating more calories but keeping your carb intake low.

If you are someone who exercises often, you can aim to add a couple hundred calories to your meal plan each day to avoid becoming overly hungry. Adding 100-200 calories to your diet on days when you are working out is a good number to aim for. The more exercise you do, the quicker you will likely see positive results. Exercise further increases your body's "fat burning" abilities and adds muscle to your frame, therefore you can get away with eating more and still be able to lose weight.

In addition to eating the right foods and the appropriate amount of carbohydrates and calories, you will want to keep these other factors in mind that can help you achieve results quickly while still making sure to do so in a healthy way:

1- Reduce stressors in your life as much as possible-

When we are stressed, our bodies release the hormone cortisol. This leads to other behavioral problems, like cravings and trouble sleeping (which we will get to in following points), but cortisol is also troublesome because it makes our bodies hold on to fat cells and not release them very easily. It's been shown that cortisol especially makes us gain weight around the belly area, which is why many people find this to be the most difficult place to tone up even though they exercise often.

Cortisol is trouble because it means you can eat roughly the same amount and types of food one year while you aren't very stressed, and you will not have any issues with weight gain, but then all of a sudden when life becomes very stressful the following year, you may find you aren't changing your eating habits much but are still gaining weight. This is due to cortisol's fat-storing effect on the body.

People experiencing a lot of stress often crave foods that make them feel more comforted, especially foods that are high in carbs, salt, sugar, and unhealthy fats. This is a natural response that the body has when undergoing stress; stress means you are experiencing a drop in "feel good" hormones like serotonin and dopamine, so your brain craves a rush of these mood boosting hormones in the form of food.

We often want foods that remind us of childhood or good periods of our lives when we are sad, frustrated, or lonely because we want to be brought back to that time period. The more stressed we are feeling, usually the less willpower we have to deal with these cravings, and so we often find ourselves giving in to these cravings. For this reason, we want to avoid stressful situations as much as possible and do things intentionally that relax us; this may include exercising more, yoga, writing in a journal, meditation, getting massages, and other techniques.

2- Make Sure You Get Enough Sleep-

A lack of sleep throws our hormones off and makes it difficult for us to tune in with our bodies and manage our hunger properly-specifically it messes with our ability to produce the hormone leptin which makes us feel full. We crave foods to boost our energy-especially sugar and carbs- because we didn't rest enough to restore our bodies.

On top of this, we are too tired to keep up with our normal exercise routines and may decide to be a bit more sedentary during stressful times, which means we should really be eating even less. Just like with cravings, stress weakens our willpower and causes us to be tired and unmotivated. Give your body enough rest: ideally 7-8 hours every night.

3- Drink Plenty of Water-

Staying hydrated is essential for proper body function and also just feeling your best. Caffeine- from sources like coffee, tea, and energy drinks-and also alcohol both dehydrate the body, so for this reason it's important to be cautious of how much you consume of both. On top of dehydrating the body, both caffeine and alcohol affect your mood, overall energy levels, sleep cycles, and cravings as well. The reason for this is because they have an impact on your hormones, which control of these feelings.

Water helps to make us feel full and also helps to eliminate toxins from our bodies.
Sometimes we may think we are hungry for more food, and we may experience food cravings, but in fact we are suffering from mild dehydration and what we actually need is more water. When we don't stay hydrated, we don't feel our best- we get tired, moody, we have headaches, and we don't function well overall. These uncomfortable feelings make us crave food because we are looking to feel better and gain more energy.

Water can help us to eat less at times too. Try drinking 2 glasses of water right before you eat a meal and you may find you actually eat a bit less. While you are eating, once you are done eating a smaller portion of food than you normally would, drink a big glass of water and wait 10 minutes; you may find that you are in fact full enough and don't need anything else.

Water also helps to "flush" our bodies clean and move food through our digestive system better. When we are dieting and switching from a bad diet to a better one, our bodies need water to help move all of the toxins we have built up in our intestines out. We are better able to go to the bathroom when we are hydrated, and this is literally how we "remove weight" from our bodies.

Low Carb Breakfast Recipes

Ham and Eggs with Vegetables

Yield: 2 Servings

Nutrition Per Serving:

Calories: 517

Fat: 42g

Protein: 23g

Carbohydrates: 12g

Fiber: 3g

Ingredients:

- ½ cup frozen peas
- 4 eggs
- 4 green olives
- ¾ cup cubed ham
- 4 tablespoon olive oil
- ½ cup chopped mushrooms
- ½ medium diced onion

Step-By-Step Instructions:

1) Place peas in microwavable bowl and add a small amount of water. Cover with a saucer and cook on high for 4 minutes.
2) Start sautéing mushrooms, onion, 2 tablespoons olive oil, and cubed ham on a medium skillet on medium-high heat until done.
3) Fry eggs and the remaining olive oil in an additional pan. Ensure it is a little runny and not completely set.
4) Stir in the peas with the ham mixture and let it all cook a few minutes longer.

5) Chop and pit the olives.
6) Divide the ham mixture onto two separate plates and top with fried eggs.
7) Add olives to taste.

 Mexican Omelette

Yield: 1 Serving

Nutrition Per Serving:

Calories: 365

Fat: 3g

Protein: 25g

Carbohydrates: 5g

Fiber: 1g

Ingredients:

- 1 tablespoon butter
- 2 ounces shredded pepper jack cheese
- 2 tablespoon salsa
- 2 eggs – beaten
- Hot sauce to taste

Step-By-Step Instructions:

1) Start by heating a skillet on medium-high heat.
2) Beat the eggs together until desired consistency.
3) Add the butter to the skillet and allow it to melt.
4) Pour eggs in skillet and allow setting to begin.
5) Add ingredients to one side of Omelette.
6) Fold over and enjoy.

 Huevos Rancheros

Yield: 1 Serving

Nutrition Per Serving:

   Calories: 355

Fat: 10g

Protein: 25g

Carbohydrates: 4g

Fiber: 1g

Ingredients:

- 1 tablespoon olive oil
- 2 eggs
- 3 tablespoon salsa
- 2 ounces shredded Monterey jack cheese

Step-By-Step Instructions:

1) Spray skillet with non-stick spray and place over medium heat.
2) Add oil to the skillet and crack eggs into skillet.
3) Turn down the heat and cover, allow eggs to fry for about 5 minutes.
4) While eggs are frying, warm salsa in an additional saucepan or microwave if you so choose.
5) When eggs are almost complete, top with cheese and add a teaspoon of water to the skillet.
6) Transfer the eggs to a plate and top with salsa, enjoy.

Ham and Cheese Puff

Yield: 4 Servings

Nutrition Per Serving:

Calories: 433

Fat: 18g

Protein: 29g

Carbohydrates: 10g

Fiber: 2g

Ingredients:

- ¼ lb ham
- ¼ lb cheddar cheese
- 1 can mushrooms, drained
- 5 eggs
- 1 green pepper

- 3 tablespoon unflavored protein powder or soy powder
- ½ teaspoon baking powder
- ½ teaspoon salt
- 1 cup small-curd cottage cheese
- 2 tablespoon grated horseradish

Step-By-Step Instructions:

1) Preheat oven to 350 F.
2) Spray 6-cup casserole dish with nonstick cooking spray.
3) Use food processor with S-blade in place to grind the ham, green pepper, mushrooms and cheddar cheese until finely chopped.
4) In large bowl beat eggs well and add protein or soy powder, baking powder, and salt, beat again.
5) Beat in cottage cheese and horseradish and add chopped ham mixture.
6) Pour egg mixture into the prepared casserole dish.
7) Bake for about 40 min or until puffy and set.

Yield: 1 Serving

Nutrition Per Serving:

> *Fat:* 8g
>
> *Protein:* 25g
>
> *Carbohydrates:* 3g
>
> *Fiber:* 1g

Ingredients:

- 3 eggs
- 2 tablespoon heavy cream
- ¼ cup grated parmesan cheese
- ½ teaspoon minced garlic
- ½ tablespoon butter
- ½ teaspoon ground rosemary

Step-By-Step Instructions:

1) Whisk eggs, cheese, cream, rosemary and garlic together in a bowl.
2) Put a medium skillet over medium-high heat.
3) Once the pan is hot, add in butter.
4) Stir the mixture prior to adding it into the skillet.
5) Scramble until eggs set, then enjoy!

Yield: 8 Servings

Nutrition Per Serving:

> *Calories:* 462

> *Fat:* 12g

> *Protein:* 17g

> *Carbohydrates:* 10g

> *Fiber:* 4g

Ingredients:

- Premade crust
- 8 ounces sliced mushrooms
- ½ cup chopped onion
- 2 tablespoon butter
- 10 ounces frozen chopped spinach – thawed
- 3 eggs

- ¾ Low fat milk
- ¾ cup heavy cream
- 2 tablespoon dry vermouth
- ½ teaspoon salt
- ¼ teaspoon pepper
- 1 ½ cup shredded Monterey Jack cheese

Step-By-Step Instructions:

1) Preaheat oven to 325 F.
2) In a large skillet over medium-high heat saute the mushrooms and onions in butter for about five minutes.
3) Move the mixture into a large mixing bowl.
4) Dump thawed spinach into a strainer and squeeze to remove as much moisture as possible. Add to mushroom mixture.
5) Add eggs, milk, and cream.
6) Whisk until a nice consistency.
7) Whisk in the vermouth, salt, and pepper.
8) Cover the bottom of the crush with the Monterey Jack and place in oven for a few minutes until the cheese begins to melt.
9) Remove from the oven and pour in the mixture.
10) Bake for 50-60 minutes and let cool.

Cauli-Kedgeree

Yield: 1 Serving

Nutrition Per Serving:

Calories: 200

Fat: 7g

Protein: 16g

Carbohydrates: 14g

Fiber: 4g

Ingredients:

- ¼ head cauliflower
- ¼ cup chopped onion
- 1 cup sliced mushroom
- ½ tablespoon butter
- ½ cup frozen green beans
- 2 hardboiled eggs

- Salt and pepper to taste

Step-By-Step Instructions:

1) Run cauliflower through shredding blade of food processor.
2) Put cauliflower in microwaveable dish and place the green beans on top. Add a few tablespoons of water and cover. Microwave on high for 6-7 minutes.
3) Saute onions and mushrooms in butter for about 5 minutes on medium-high.
4) Peel eggs and cut into quarters.
5) When microwave mixture is complete, drain and stir into the mushroom mixture.
6) Add salt and pepper to taste.
7) Place eggs on top and enjoy.

Hot Coconut-Almond Cereal

Yield: 1 Serving

Nutrition Per Serving:

    Calories: 379

    Fat: 25g

    Protein: 27g

    Carbohydrates: 19g

    Fiber: 10g

If you enjoy cereal, but you are avoiding it due to the carbs, avoid it no more. This delicious cereal is exactly what you're looking for. Served hot, this cereal maybe should be considered more of an oatmeal, but not as bland. The flavor is great and the best part, it only takes a few minutes to prepare.

Ingredients:

    -    2 tablespoons almond meal

- 2 tablespoons flax seed meal
- 1 tablespoon finely shredded coconut meat
- 1 tablespoon vanilla whey protein powder
- 1 pinch of salt
- 1 tablespoon almond butter
- ⅓ cup boiling water

Step-By-Step Instructions:

1) Spoon the flax seed meal, almond meal, whey protein, coconut, and salt in a bowl and stir.
2) Add the almond butter and boiling water – stir until butter is melted.
3) Serve with sweetener to taste (optional)

Tomato & Cheese Omelette

Yield: 1 Serving

Nutrition Per Serving:

Calories: 285

Fat: 7g

Protein: 20g

Carbohydrates: 5g

Fiber: 1g

If you are looking for a quick, easy, and high protein option for the morning, this is a great dish. Omelets don't take long to assemble, and they taste fantastic. If you like tomatoes and mozzarella, give this a shot!

Ingredients:

- 2 eggs – beaten
- ⅓ cup shredded mozzarella cheese
- 2 tablespoons fresh basil – chopped

- ½ small tomato – sliced

Step-By-Step Instructions:

1) Preheat your skillet on medium heat, make sure it's hot before proceeding. If it is non-stick don't worry about spray, otherwise ensure it is greased.
2) Pour in eggs and proceed making omelet.
3) Cover half the omelet with cheese and tomatoes.
4) Cover the skillet, put burner on low, and let the cheese melt for 2-3 minutes.
5) Top the omelet with basil if you so choose, and serve.

 Salmon Scramble

Yield: 3 Servings

Nutrition Per Serving:

Calories: 292

Fat: 8g

Protein: 27g

Carbohydrates: 5g

Fiber: 1g

If you enjoy salmon and eggs, by god you have to try this dish. It is a perfect mix of the two and it takes little time to make. If you're looking for a light, but protein-rich breakfast, you'll enjoy this.

Ingredients:

-   4 eggs
-   ½ cup heavy cream
-   1 teaspoon dried dill weed

- ¼ lb goat cheese (chevre)
- ¼ lb moist smoked salmon
- 4 scallions
- 1 tablespoon butter

Step-By-Step Instructions:

1) Whisk together the eggs, cream and dill weed.
2) Slice the scallions thin, you may include part of the green if you choose.
3) Cut the goat cheese up into small pieces.
4) Crumble the salmon.
5) In a non-stick skillet (large), melt the butter over medium-high heat.
6) Add scallions and sauté for a minute.
7) Add egg mixture and cook, ensure you stir frequently. When they're halfway set (1.5 minutes) add the goat cheese and salmon.
8) Stir until eggs are set, and serve!

Low Carb Lunches

Yield: 2

Nutrition Per Serving:

> *Calories:* 400
>
> *Fat:* 7g
>
> *Protein:* 38g

Carbohydrates: 25g

Lettuce or collard wraps are the perfect way to get that sandwich feeling, without any carbs at all. Use the same idea in multiple ways, such as for teriyaki or Greek salad wraps.

Ingredients:

- 2 large collard wraps, or another lettuce like Boston or Bibb lettuce
- 2 chicken breasts
- 1 cup of tomato sauce (or more if you'd like)
- 1 bunch of broccoli raab
- ½ cup jarred roasted red peppers
- 1 eggplant
- 2 oz. good quality cheese of your choice (fontina, asiago, parm, etc.)

Step-By-Step Instructions:

1) Cook chicken in a sauté pan with olive oil until browned and cooked through, about 8-9 minutes, then remove from pan.
2) Chop up rinsed broccoli raab and eggplant and add to a sauté pan with olive oil. Cook for about 8-9 minutes.
3) Lay out collard wraps and add tomato sauce on top, then broccoli, red peppers, and cheese. You may wish to microwave for 30 seconds or put into oven to melt the cheese.

Yield: 2

Nutrition Per Serving:

Calories: 400

Fat: 17g

Protein: 28g

Carbohydrates: 19g

Herbs and lemon give fish instant flavor instant. Serve with as many vegetables as you'd like and make extra lemon & herb sauce for dressing.

Ingredients:

- 2 pieces of halibut (could sub for sea bass, cod, halibut etc.)
- 1 bunch of carrots, peeled (about 4 carrots)
- 1 avocado, pit rem

- Fresh chopped herbs (parsley, dill, oregano)
- 2 tomatoes
- Premade salad mix
- Salt & pepper
- Olive oil

Step-By-Step Instructions:

1) Cut up the peeled carrots and put them onto a baking pan with olive oil. Roast them in 400 degree oven for about 35 minutes, flipping half way through.
2) Spray another pan with cooking spray and add your halibut. Flip once its turning pink around the sides, about 6 minutes. Cook for another 5 minutes on the other side.
3) Mix together your carrots, tomatoes, and avocado. Serve alongside fish drizzled with lemon juice. Add herbs and more oil on top for more flavor if you'd like.

Stuffed Zucchini Boats

Yield: 2

Nutrition Per Serving:

Calories: 380

Fat: 3g

Protein: 33g

Carbohydrates: 22g

The perfect thing to make when you are craving pizza!

Ingredients:

- 1 large zucchini, cut in half
- 1 large onion, chopped finely
- 2 peppers (I'd recommend a mix of colors), chopped finely
- 1 cup chopped turkey/chicken meat
- 1 cup of marinara sauce
- ½ cup mozzarella cheese
- (Optional) fresh herbs- I used parsley & oregano

Step-By-Step Instructions:

1) Cook chopped meat in a sauté pan coated in olive oil, about 10 minutes or until browned.
2) In a separate bowl at the same time, cook zucchini halves, onions and peppers for about 8 minutes.
3) Top zucchini halves with tomato sauce, meat, veggie mixture and herbs, cheese and melt in microwave or oven, then serve.

Blackened Cod with Ratatouille

Yield: 2

Nutrition Per Serving:

Calories: 400

Fat: 4g

Protein: 27g

Carbohydrates: 22g

Cod is a flaky white fish that most people enjoy, but feel free to sub in another fish filet if you'd like.

Ingredients:

- 2 filets of cod
- 1 eggplant, chopped into cubes
- 1 pepper, chopped
- 1 onion, finely chopped
- 1 zucchini, finely chopped
- Tomato sauce (optional)

Step-By-Step Instructions:

1) Cook cod filets in a sauté pan coated in olive oil, about 5 minutes on each side.
2) At the same time, in a separate big pan cook all your chopped vegetables for 10 minutes in a little olive oil. Add tomato sauce if you are using it.
3) Serve both together.

Salad with Brussel Sprouts, Grilled Chicken, and Summer Squash

Yield: 1 Salad

Nutrition Per Serving:

> *Calories:* 450
>
> *Fat:* 18g
>
> *Protein:* 30g
>
> *Carbohydrates:* 10g

Brussel sprouts have a flavor that really pops when roasted. If you have the extra time, it's worth popping them into the oven for 30 minutes. If not, shred raw sprouts in a food processor and serve as a shredded salad.

Ingredients:

- 1 small summer squash, chopped (or sub for butternut, spaghetti, etc.)
- 1 lb. Brussels sprouts (rinsed and dried)
- 2 tablespoons nuts (pistachios, sliced almonds, diced walnuts)
- 1-2 tablespoons of dressing that you'd like
- 1 chicken breast, grilled

Step-By-Step Instructions:

1) Put Brussels sprouts on a flat baking pan and sprinkle with olive oil. Roast in 400 degree oven for 35 minutes, flipping half way through.
2) Put a little olive oil into a sauté pan and add chopped squash. Cook for about 8 minutes or until soft.
3) Cut up cooked chicken breast into small pieces and mix with Brussel sprouts and squash. Then top with nuts and dressing and serve.

"Bunless" Easy Homemade Veggie Burgers

Yield: 6 burgers

Nutrition Per Serving:

Calories: 400

Fat: 19g

Protein: 19g

Carbohydrates: 18g

A filling, nutty burger that can topped with any of your favorite choices

Ingredients:

- 1 cup almond meal
- 1 large onion, chopped
- 6 large carrots, car
- 3 tablespoons tomato paste
- 2 packages button mushrooms, wiped clean and chopped
- 1 cup walnuts crushed up finely

- (Optional) spices to taste- rosemary, oregano, thyme,

Step-By-Step Instructions:

1) Add olive oil to a large pan and sauté the onions, carrots, and mushrooms until browned, about 4 minutes.
2) Add the tomato paste and continue to cook, stirring constantly, for another 1 minute.
3) Add the cooked veggies, walnuts, and almond meal to a big bowl and mash together. Then make into patties on sauté in a pan on each side for about 3 minutes or until browned.

Grilled Citrus Shrimp over Summer Salad

Yield: 4

Nutrition Per Serving:

Calories: 300

Fat: 5g

Protein: 26g

Carbohydrates: 18g

Shrimp are a great high protein, low carb food to make in a pinch. Keep them in your freezer so you know you have a protein option when something fresh isn't available

Ingredients:

- 1 lb. shrimp (you could also use scallops)
- 2 lemons
- 1 large orange
- 1 lb. cherry tomatoes

- 1 large cucumber
- 1 red onion
- Premade salad (from a bag)
- Or make salad with 8 cups greens, carrots, radishes

Step-By-Step Instructions:

1) Grill your shrimp in a sauté pan with a little olive oil, about 3 minutes on each side or until pink.
2) Toss your cooked shrimp in juice from the lemons and orange, then "zest" your orange skin and add zest to the bowl.
3) Top your salad with cut up veggies and shrimp mixture and serve.

Kale Salad with Steak, Green Beans, and Almonds

Yield: 4

Nutrition Per Serving:

Calories: 450

Fat: 19g

Protein: 35g

Carbohydrates: 18g

Kale is a nutritional power house, and the addition of steak and almonds makes this salad extra filling.

Ingredients:

- 4 servings of steak (whichever cut you'd like, flank steak is recommended)
- 8 cups Kale, washed and chopped
- 1 lb. green beans
- 1 cup slivered almonds
- 4 tablespoons of premade salad dressing

- Tomatoes, onion, cucumbers (optional)

Step-By-Step Instructions:

1) Grill your steak in a sauté pan then slice thinly.
2) Add green beans to the pan after and cook for about 7 minutes or until softened.
3) Chop kale finely and toss in dressing. Then add steak, almonds, and green beans on top of the salad and serve.

Southwestern Chicken Burgers (Bunless)

Yield: 4

Nutrition Per Serving:

Calories: 300

Fat: 4g

Protein: 30g

Carbohydrates: 18g

A spicy Tex-Mex take on regular chicken burgers, great for keeping things interesting

Ingredients:

- 1 lb. ground chicken
- 1 large red onion
- 2 peppers

- ½ cup whole wheat or panko breadcrumbs
- 1 taco seasoning mix packet
- Salad to serve with burgers, or wrap them in lettuce "wraps"

Step-By-Step Instructions:

1) Brown chicken in a sauté pan with olive oil until cooked through, about 10 minutes.
2) Mash cooked chicken and chopped up veggies together either in a food processor or by hand and form into patties.
3) Pan Fry each side in a little bit of olive oil in a sauté pan, then serve over salad.

Yield: 1 protein shake

Nutrition Per Serving:

      Calories: 400

      Fat: 15g

      Protein: 13g

      Carbohydrates: 17g

A filling delicious smoothie to take along with you when you're short on time

Ingredients:

- ½ cup blueberries (or other low sugar fruit)
- 1 tablespoon peanut butter/almond butter
- 1-2 tablespoon raw cocoa powder (unsweetened)
- 2 tablespoons flax/chia seeds
- 1-2 cups almond/other nut milk
- (Optional) a little bit of very cold water to thin it out or ice

Step-By-Step Instructions:

1) Blend everything together and enjoy!

Tuna Steak with Tomatoes and High-Protein Pesto Sauce

Yield: 2

Nutrition Per Serving:

> *Calories:* 400
>
> *Fat:* 14g
>
> *Protein:* 28g
>
> *Carbohydrates:* 2g

Basic tuna becomes extra delicious when topped with a simple pesto sauce. This same sauce could be used over chicken or any fish.

Ingredients:

- 2 tuna steaks
- 2 oz. parmesan cheese
- 1 cup packed basil, washed and chopped

- 1 lemon, juiced
- 3 tablespoons olive oil
- Water to thin sauce out if you need
- 2 garlic cloves (optional)

Step-By-Step Instructions:

1) Cook tuna in a sauté pan coated in olive oil, about 5 minutes on each side, only until starting to turn pink.
2) At the same time, in a food processor put all other ingredients in for the pesto and blend until smooth (lemon juice, garlic, basil, cheese, water plus salt, pepper). Taste to make sure it doesn't need more salt, pepper, or lemon.
3) Serve tuna steaks with pesto sauce on top. Add a side salad or more vegetables if you'd like.

"Breakfast for Lunch": Poached Eggs and Bacon with Herbs and Savory Veggies

Yield: 2

Nutrition Per Serving:

Calories: 300

Fat: 10g

Protein: 25g

Carbohydrates: 15g

An easy option for "bacon and eggs for dinner". Eggs are a great staple to keep in your kitchen because of how long they last.

Ingredients:

- 4 organic cage-free eggs
- 4 strips of bacon
- 2 peppers
- 1 medium onion

- 2 tomatoes
- Fresh herbs- I used parsley & oregano
- Olive oil

Step-By-Step Instructions:

1) Spray a pan with cooking spray/some olive oil and add your onions first for a few minutes, then add peppers & tomatoes. Cook until everything is browned, about 6 minutes.
2) Wipe pan clean and cook bacon until cooked through.
3) Add your fresh herbs and veggies back to the pan with bacon and toss around. Create little wells in your vegetable mixture and drop eggs into the holes. Cook until eggs are firm and finished, about 4-6 more minutes.

Low Carb Dinner Recipes

Mahi Mahi with Broccoli Slaw

Yield: 2

Nutrition Per Serving:

> *Calories:* 320

> *Fat:* 9g

> *Protein:* 32g

> *Carbohydrates:* 12g

A take on fish tacos, only without the corn tortilla shell. You can make these into foldable "tacos" using lettuce wraps if you'd like to.

Ingredients:

- 2 fish filets (cod, Mahi Mahi, or other white fish)
- 1 package of premade coleslaw mix
- 1 package of shredded broccoli
- 1 1/2 cup salsa (try mango, peach, or pineapple salsa if you'd like)
- 4 lettuce/collard wraps if you wish to make them into "tacos"

Step-By-Step Instructions:

1) Grill your fish filets in a sauté pan until flaky on both sides, then slice thinly.
2) Mix your coleslaw, broccoli, and salsa together in a big bowl.
3) Top lettuce "taco" wraps with fish and coleslaw mixture, add extra salsa if you'd like.

Kale Salad with Avocado and Shrimp

Yield: 2

Nutrition Per Serving:

Calories: 400

Fat: 16g

Protein: 27g

Carbohydrates: 11g

The protein from shrimp and healthy fats from avocado make this extra filling. Sub the shrimp for any other fish or shellfish that you'd like.

Ingredients:

- 4 cups kale, cut into strips
- 1 avocado, peeled and cut into cubes
- 12 large shrimp, thawed and cleaned
- ½ large red onion, cut into thin slices
- Salad dressing of your choice

Step-By-Step Instructions:

1) Cook shrimp in a sauté pan until pink on both sides, only about 7 minutes total.
2) Add shrimp, avocado, red onion slices, and dressing onto salad and mix together, then serve. Add any other vegetables on the side that you'd like.

Eggplant "Parmesan"

Yield: 2

Nutrition Per Serving:

    Calories: 400

    Fat: 14g

    Protein: 14g

    Carbohydrates: 18g

Skip the high carb Italian bread and breadcrumbs and instead using almond meal to create the same type of breaded coating, only a lot healthier!

Ingredients:

- 1 large eggplant, cut into flat big slices
- 1/2 cup almond meal
- 2 oz. mozzarella cheese
- 1 cup crushed seasoned tomatoes
- Fresh basil
- (optional) salad or eggplant and zucchini to serve with this

Step-By-Step Instructions:

1) Dip eggplant slices in almond meal and then add them to sauté pan and cook on both sides for about 4-5 minutes or until soft and browned.
2) Top eggplant slices with tomato sauce, cheese, basil and serve.

Chicken and Vegetable Fajitas

Yield: 2

Nutrition Per Serving:

> *Calories:* 400
>
> *Fat:* 10g
>
> *Protein:* 27g
>
> *Carbohydrates:* 20g

Get your Mexican fix without all the unnecessary carbs from rice and beans. Fill up on the guacamole, vegetables, and chicken instead.

Ingredients:

- 2 chicken breasts
- 2 peppers
- 1 medium onion
- 1 cup salsa
- 1 packet fajita seasoning
- 1 avocado or 1 cup premade guacamole

Step-By-Step Instructions:

1) Cook chicken in a sauté pan coated in olive oil, about 5 minutes on each side, then slice into strips.
2) At the same time, in a separate big pan cook all your chopped onion and peppers with fajitas seasoning.
3) Serve chicken and vegetables with salsa and avocado.

 Spinach Salad with Hard Boiled Eggs, Avocado, and String Beans

Yield: 1

Nutrition Per Serving:

Calories: 400

Fat: 22g

Protein: 20g

Carbohydrates: 10g

Making a big batch of hard boiled eggs ahead of time is a great way to keep an easy source of instant protein and fat on hand for when you're busy. Use any other lettuce or vegetable if you don't have spinach and green beans.

Ingredients:

- 2 hard boiled organic cage-free eggs
- 2-3 cups spinach, washed and chopped

- ½ avocado, chopped into cubs
- 1 ½ cups green beans
- Oil based of your choice
- Any other vegetables you'd like to add

Step-By-Step Instructions:

1) Boil green beans for about 8 minutes, or use defrosted frozen green beans.
2) Peel pre-hard boiled eggs and cut into slivers, then add to spinach salad (if you need to boil eggs, put into cold water and bring to boil, then let them sit for 13 minutes covered in pot).
3) Add avocado, green beans, and dressing to salad and toss everything together, then serve.

Turkey, Brie, and Apple "Wraps"

Yield: 2

Nutrition Per Serving:

Calories: 400

Fat: 7g

Protein: 22g

Carbohydrates: 11g

The perfect quick dinner to make when you're craving a turkey sandwich. You could create a similar meal by using a no sugar-added cranberry sauce on top of the turkey slices to create a "thanksgiving" feeling dinner.

Ingredients:

- 2 collard wraps
- 2 servings of organic sliced turkey or chicken breast
- 1 green apple
- 2 tablespoons of ground mustard
- 2 servings of sharp cheese like fontina or cheddar
- 1 bag premade salad

Step-By-Step Instructions:

1) Chop apple into flat slice.
2) Lay out wrap then top with mustard, turkey, apples, and cheese.
3) Serve with side salad.

Pistachio, Herb and Lemon Crusted Salmon with Salad

Yield: 2

Nutrition Per Serving:

Calories: 400

Fat: 17g

Protein: 32g

Carbohydrates: 8g

If you aren't a fan of salmon, feel free to sub in another more mild fish. The coating would also work using walnuts, macadamia nuts, or almond meal.

Ingredients:

- 2 pieces of Salmon (wild)
- ½ cup crushed/ground pistachios
- 1 lemon, juiced
- A bunch of fresh herbs (dill, parsley recommended)
- 1 bag premade salad
- Olive oil

Step-By-Step Instructions:

1) Pour lemon juice over salmon filets and then roll them in ground pistachios and cut up herbs.
2) Sear them in a sauté pan on both sides until flaky and cooked through, about 10 minutes.
3) Serve with premade salad and drizzle with more olive oil or dressing and fresh herbs.

Salad with Strawberries, Walnuts, and Grilled Chicken

Yield: 1

Nutrition Per Serving:

>*Calories:* 425

>*Fat:* 18

>*Protein:* 32g

>*Carbohydrates:* 18g

A light salad that has the perfect mixture of protein, fat, something crunchy, and something sweet.

Ingredients:

- 1 bag premade spinach salad
- ½ cup fresh strawberries, rinsed and chopped
- ¼ cup walnuts

- 1 chicken breast
- 1 tablespoons of balsamic vinaigrette dressing
- ½ cup canned hearts of palms (artichoke hearts)
- Any other vegetables you'd like

Step-By-Step Instructions:

1) Grill chicken in a sauté pan with some olive oil or cooking spray, then slice it add it on top of salad.
2) Top salad with berries, hearts of palm, walnuts, and dressing then serve.

Salmon Burgers with Grilled Asparagus

Yield: 2

Nutrition Per Serving:

>*Calories:* 360

>*Fat:* 12g

>*Protein:* 27g

>*Carbohydrates:* 11g

You can find many types of frozen seafood burgers in most grocery stores or health food stores. Just check ingredients for added bread crumbs or fillers. Try making your own salmon burgers using canned salmon and almond meal instead of breadcrumbs.

Ingredients:

- 2 premade store-bought salmon burgers (look in freezer aisle)

- 1 lb. asparagus, cleaned and trimmed
- 1 lemon
- 2 large tomatoes
- Premade salad mix (would recommend baby spring mix)
- Fresh herbs (dill, thyme, parsley)
- Olive oil based dressing
- Any other vegetables you'd like to add

Step-By-Step Instructions:

1) Add olive oil to a large pan and warm up the burgers on both sides, about 8 minutes.
2) In a separate grill pan, sauté the asparagus until soft and cooked, about 8 minutes.
3) Top finished burgers with sliced tomato and chopped fresh herbs.
4) Serve alongside asparagus drizzled with lemon juice and olive oil.

Spicy Tex-Mex Chicken Soup

Yield: 2

Nutrition Per Serving:

> *Calories:* 380
>
> *Fat:* 5g
>
> *Protein:* 25g
>
> *Carbohydrates:* 18g

Skip store-bought soups that usually have carb fillers such as pasta or gluten added. Make your own in a big pot and keep leftovers frozen for future meals.

Ingredients:

- 2 chicken breasts
- 1 pepper
- 1 onion
- 1 can seasoned tomato sauce (look for the kind with chilies and garlic)
- Some water/stock to thin out sauce
- (Optional) add other vegetables that you'd like

Step-By-Step Instructions:

1) Grill your chicken in a sauté pan with a little olive oil, about 5 minutes on each side or until cooked, then slice thinly.
2) In a separate pan, cook onions and peppers until soft, then add in tomato sauce.
3) Add beans and chicken to vegetables and stir everything together, then serve.

Chicken Marsala with Broccoli

Yield: 2

Nutrition Per Serving:

> *Calories:* 400

> *Fat:* 4

> *Protein:* 27g

> *Carbohydrates:* 10g

An old restaurant favorite made low carb. Add as many mushrooms, onions, and other vegetables as you'd like. Also top with cheese for even more filling protein if you wish.

Ingredients:

- 2 chicken breasts
- 1 lb. of mushrooms, washed and chopped
- 1 head broccoli, washed and chopped (or use frozen)
- 1 onion, chopped finely
- ½ cup Marsala cooking wine
- Olive oil
- (Optional) cheese for melting on top

Step-By-Step Instructions:

1) Add olive oil to a sauté pan and cook your chicken on both sides, about 5 minutes each.
2) In separate pan at the same time, cook mushrooms, broccoli and onions for about 10 minutes with Marsala wine added for last 5 minutes.
3) Serve cooked vegetables poured over chicken, add fresh herbs or melted cheese if you'd like.

Turkey Bolognese Stuffed Spaghetti Squash

Yield: 2

Nutrition Per Serving:

Calories: 400

Fat: 8

Protein: 28g

Carbohydrates: 17g

Spaghetti squash is low carb and low calorie, making it the perfect sub for pasta when you have the craving. Use the squash "noodles" in various ways wherever you normally would add macaroni.

Ingredients:

- 1 jar tomato marinara sauce
- 2 servings chopped good quality turkey meat or regular chopped meat (preferably organic)
- 1 spaghetti squash, cut in half
- 1 lb. mushrooms, chopped
- 1 onion, chopped finely
- Fresh herbs (basil, oregano, parsley)
- Olive oil
- (optional) cheese to melt

Step-By-Step Instructions:

1) Microwave your squash in a microwave safe bowl for 8-9 minutes or until cooked through.
2) While squash is cooking, cook chopped meat, mushrooms and onions in a sauté pan with a little olive oil until browned and soft, about 8 minutes.
3) Scoop out squash "strands" once cooled a bit and mix with all other ingredients, then add your "pasta" mixture

back into squash halves. Melt cheese on top and add fresh herbs if you'd like before serving.

Delicious Veggies

Oven Roasted Vegetables

Yield: 4 Servings

Nutrition Per Serving:

> *Protein:* 3.6g
>
> *Carbohydrates:* 7.3g

These are great for a quick snack, especially if you are not hitting your daily veggie intake. The carbohydrates in this recipe are good carbs and fine for you to eat almost as many as you want. If there is a veggie not listed, feel free to add it, the more the merrier!

Ingredients:

- 1 red bell pepper – cut into strips
- 1 cup mushrooms – halved
- ½ bulb fennel – cut into triangles
- 20 spears asparagus
- 4 shallots – peeled

- 4 cloves garlic -- peeled
- Olive oil for coating
- Salt and pepper to taste

Step-By-Step Instructions:

1) Preheat oven to 450 Degrees Fahrenheit
2) Toss vegetables in olive oil to coat.
3) Season with salt and pepper to taste.
4) Spread on baking sheet and place in oven for 15 minutes at 450.
5) Reduce heat to 375 after the 15 minutes elapses.
6) Depending on how you enjoy your veggies, they should be done in about 45 minutes total. The asparagus is usually one of the first veggies to finish, feel free to remove these if the rest of the veggies have not finished cooking.

Broccoli Heads with Garlic and Parm

Yield: 4 servings

Nutrition Per Serving:

Protein: 4.2g

Carbohydrates: 2.75g

If you are sick of the same old steamed broccoli, this may be a good option for you. The garlic and parmesan cheese complement the broccoli to make a delicious combination. Feeling a bit adventurous? Give this a try.

Ingredients:

- 2 cups broccoli florets (just the heads of broccoli)
- 3 tablespoons olive oil
- 2 garlic cloves – minced
- Salt and pepper to taste
- ¼ cup freshly grated parmesan cheese

- 2 tablespoons chopped basil

Step-By-Step Instructions:

1) Cook the broccoli in the microwave for about 30 seconds until the coloring turns bright green.
2) Heat olive oil in skillet and sauté garlic for two minutes.
3) Add broccoli to the mixture and stir around to coat it completely.
4) Sauté for 3-5 minutes until broccoli is to your liking.
5) Season with salt and pepper to your liking and toss with parmesan & basil.

Spaghetti Squash

Yield: 8 servings

Nutrition Per Serving:

Protein: .7g

Carbohydrates: 5.85g

Spaghetti squash is a delicious low carb replacement for real pasta. It is best served with a nice white mushroom cream sauce or clam sauce. That doesn't mean it has to be served as a pasta, it is also very good on its own, go ahead and give this one a try.

Ingredients:

- A medium spaghetti squash (2-3lbs)
- Salt and pepper to taste
- Olive oil

Step-By-Step Instructions:

1) Boil squash in water completely covered for 30 minutes, or until the skin is tender.
2) Remove seeds and stringy center from the squash.
3) Scoop out the flesh & toss with salt, pepper and olive oil.
4) It is ready to be served, but if you want, add some grated cheese to taste.

Parm-Crusted Zucchini

Yield: 2 servings

Nutrition Per Serving:

Protein: 20g

Carbohydrates: 5.75g

This is a fantastic protein packed snack. If you are fan of parmesan cheese and you need a nice protein-rich veggie, this is a great option. At 20g of protein per serving, you can forget the meat in your meal if you wish, but I wouldn't!

Ingredients:

- 2 small zucchini – cut into ¼ inch slices
- 1 egg – slightly beaten
- ¾ cup freshly grated parmesan cheese
- 1 cup olive oil
- Salt and pepper to taste

Step-By-Step Instructions:

1) Salt the zucchini and place on a paper towel for about 15 minutes to reduce the moisture.
2) Heat oil in the skillet until it simmers.
3) Blot zucchini dry, dip in egg, then dip in parmesan on both sides.
4) Fry zucchini slices in the oil until golden brown.
5) Let the zucchini drain on a paper towel. Add salt and pepper to taste.

Sautéed Pine Nut & Garlic Spinach

Yield: 4 servings

Nutrition Per Serving:

Protein: 3.9g

Carbohydrates: 4.9g

This is a delicious side that goes great with fish. I frequently will cook this, create a nice bed with it, and place a seared salmon on top. The protein to carb ratio is fantastic and the nutrients from the spinach are highly desired by your body.

Ingredients:

- 1 lb fresh spinach – washed
- 2 tablespoons pine nuts – toasted & lightly salted (if desired)
- 2 tablespoons olive oil
- 1 clove garlic – peeled and finely chopped
- Salt and Pepper to Taste

Step-By-Step Instructions:

1) Heat olive oil in skillet over medium heat.
2) Sauté the garlic until lightly browned, which will take about 2 minutes.
3) Add in spinach and sauté until wilted, which will take about 10 minutes.
4) Add pine nuts, stir for even distribution.
5) Add salt and pepper to taste.

Mouthwatering Desserts

Yield: 8 Servings

Nutrition Per Serving:

> *Protein:* 4.8g

> *Carbohydrates:* 3.42g

This is one of my weaknesses because I love pie, and I absolutely love peanut butter. This treat is nice and sweet, and it makes eight servings. Although I recommend sharing, I've been known to consume an entire pie to myself over the course of a few days... I hope you enjoy this as much as I do.

Ingredients:

- 2 tablespoons butter – melted
- 4 ounces cream cheese – softened
- ¾ cup pecan pieces
- 2 ½ tablespoons peanut butter

- 1 teaspoon vanilla extract
- Sweetener to taste (stevia)
- ½ cup heavy cream – whipped

Step-By-Step Instructions:

1) Grind the nuts up in a food processor and mix with the butter.
2) Press into 7 inch pie pan
3) Mix together the cream cheese, vanilla, peanut butter, and sweetener using a mixer or food processor until well-blended.
4) Fold in whipped cream.
5) Transfer the mixture to the pie pan containing the crust
6) Place in the refrigerator for 2-3 hours and then serve.

Yield: 4 servings

Nutrition Per Serving:

Protein: 6g

Carbohydrates: 4.6g

This is a nice dish near the holidays with the ginger cinnamon taste. It tastes just like a nice gingerbread cookie on Christmas. I appreciate this dessert a lot, although I don't consume it often, it is one that I highly recommend.

Ingredients:

- 2 eggs
- 2 cups heavy cream
- 3 tablespoons Da Vinci sugar-free gingerbread syrup
- ½ teaspoon vanilla extract
- ½ teaspoon cinnamon
- Dash of Salt

Step-By-Step Instructions

1) Preheat your oven to 350 Degrees Fahrenheit.
2) Beat eggs with a mixer. Mix in the cream once eggs are beaten.
3) Slowly mix in the remaining ingredients.
4) Pour into four 4-ounce custard cups.
5) Bake in a water bath for 30 minutes or until firm in the middle.

Yield: 7 Servings (3 Cookies/Serving)

Nutrition Per Serving:

Protein: 10.6g

Carbohydrates: 7.67

Although the word "cookie" typically has a negative connotation, it doesn't really apply to this recipe. These peanut butter cookies are packed with a punch of protein and they're quite tasty too! Give these a try if you're looking to add a good amount of protein into your diet.

Ingredients:

- 2 eggs
- 1 cup **natural** peanut butter
- 4 tablespoons Da Vinci sugar-free vanilla syrup
- 1 teaspoon vanilla extract
- 21 toasted peanuts – halved

Step-By-Step Instructions

1) Preheat your oven to 350 degrees Fahrenheit.
2) Beat the eggs and slowly mix in the peanut butter – stir well.
3) Add in the syrup and vanilla.
4) Place 1 table spoon mounds of cookie dough on greased baking sheet in rows – about two inches apart.
5) Add a peanut to the top of each cookie.
6) Bake for 10 minutes or until desired doneness. Makes a total of **21 cookies.**

 Walnutters

Yield: 6 servings

Nutrition Per Serving:

Protein: 2.88g

Carbohydrates: 2.06g

Walnuts have always been a favorite of mine. They go so well in desserts, but they also taste splendid alone. This recipe is really simple, has a subtly sweet and satisfying taste, and takes no time to make. If you need to cure a sweet tooth quickly, this may be the right recipe for you.

Ingredients:

- 1 cup walnut halves
- 2 tablespoon melted butter (optional)
- ¼ teaspoon cinnamon
- Salt to taste
- 2 tablespoons Da Vinci sugar-free vanilla syrup

Step-By-Step Instructions

1) Preheat your oven to 350 degrees Fahrenheit.
2) Toss walnuts in syrup and butter (if desired) until completely coated.
3) Sprinkle with salt and cinnamon to taste.
4) Bake in the oven for about 10 minutes, or until toasted.

Vanilla Cream Soda

Yield: -

Nutrition Per Serving:

Protein: >1g

Carbohydrates: 1g

This is a nice refreshing dessert drink to enjoy during the summer. It is cold and muggy, and it tastes just the right amount of sweet.

Ingredients:

- Club soda
- 2 tablespoons Da Vinci sugar-free vanilla syrup
- 2 tablespoons heavy cream

Step-By-Step Instructions

1) Fill a large glass with ice (I prefer using a frozen mug).
2) Add club soda, but leave room for syrup and cream.
3) Add syrup, stir.
4) Add cream and enjoy.

30 Day Schedule

Week One

	Breakfast	Lunch	Dinner
Day 1	Ham and Eggs with Veggies	Chicken and Roasted Veggie Wrap	Mahi Mahi with Broccoli Slaw
Day 2	Mexican omelette	Lemon halibut salad with roasted carrots	Kale Salad with Avocado and Shrimp
Day 3	Huevos rancheros	Stuffed zucchini boats	Eggplant Parm
Day 4	Ham and cheese puff	Blackened cod with ratatouille	Chicken and Vegetable Fajitas
Day 5	Parmesan & rosemary eggs	Salad with brussels sprouts, grilled chicken, and summer squash	Spinach Salad with Eggs, Avocado, and String Beans
Day 6	Spinach & mushroom quiche	Bunless easy homemade veggie burgers	Turkey, brie and apple wraps
Day 7	Cauli-kedgeree	Grilled citrus shrimp over summer salad	Pistachio, herb and lemon crusted salmon with salad

Week Two

	Breakfast	Lunch	Dinner
Day 1	Hot coconut-almond cereal	Kale salad with steak, green beans, and almonds	Salad with strawberries, walnuts, and grilled chicken
Day 2	Tomato & cheese omelette	Southwestern chicken burgers	Salmon burgers with grilled asparagus
Day 3	Salmon scramble	On-the-go protein shake	Spicy tex-mex chicken soup
Day 4	Ham and Eggs with Veggies	Tuna steak with tomatoes and high-protein pesto	Chicken marsala with broccoli
Day 5	Mexican omelette	Breakfast for lunch – poached eggs and bacon with herbs and veggies	Turkey Bolognese stuffed spaghetti squash
Day 6	Huevos rancheros	Chicken and Roasted Veggie Wrap	Mahi Mahi with broccoli slaw
Day 7	Ham and cheese puff	Lemon halibut salad with roasted carrots	Kale salad with avocado and shrimp

Week Three

	Breakfast	Lunch	Dinner
Day 1	Parmesan & rosemary eggs	Stuffed zucchini boats	Eggplant parm
Day 2	Spinach & mushroom quiche	Blackened cod with ratatouille	Chicken and vegetable fajitas
Day 3	Cauli-kedgeree	Salad with brussels sprouts, grilled chicken, and summer squash	Spinach salad with hard boiled eggs, avocado, and string beans
Day 4	Hot coconut-almond cereal	Bunless easy homemade veggie burgers	Turkey, brie, and apple wraps
Day 5	Tomato & cheese omelette	Grilled citrus shrimp over summer salad	Pistachio, herb, and lemon crusted salmon with salad
Day 6	Salmon scramble	Kale salad with steak, green beans, and almonds	Salad with strawberries, walnuts, and grilled chicken
Day 7	Ham and Eggs with Veggies	Southwestern chicken burgers	Salmon burgers with grilled asparagus

Week Four

	Breakfast	Lunch	Dinner
Day 1	Mexican omelette	On-the-go protein shake	Spicy tex-mex chicken soup
Day 2	Huevos rancheros	Tuna steak with tomatoes and high-protein pesto	Chicken marsala with broccoli
Day 3	Ham and cheese puff	Breakfast for lunch – poached eggs and bacon with herbs and veggies	Turkey Bolognese stuffed spaghetti squash
Day 4	Parmesan & rosemary eggs	Chicken and Roasted Veggie Wrap	Mahi Mahi with broccoli slaw
Day 5	Spinach & mushroom quiche	Lemon halibut salad with roasted carrots	Chicken and vegetable fajitas
Day 6	Cauli-kedgeree	Salad with brussels sprouts, grilled chicken, and summer squash	Turkey, brie, and apple wraps
Day 7	Hot coconut-almond cereal	Bunless easy homemade veggie burgers	Kale salad with avocado and shrimp

Further Reading:

For more information on low carb diets, you may want to check out these resources and websites:

http://www.atkins.com/Home.aspx

http://www.atkins.com/program/phase-1/what-you-can-eat-in-this-phase.aspx

http://www.webmd.com/diet/features/down-low-on-low-carb-diets

http://www.webmd.com/diet/features/down-low-on-low-carb-diets

"The Ketogenic Diet". http://www.ketogenic-diet-resource.com/